1967



3-7-17

# HUMANISM AND THEOLOGY

# PUBLISHED AQUINAS LECTURES

*St. Thomas and the Life of Learning* (1937) by the Rev. John F. McCormick, S.J., former professor of philosophy at Loyola University.

*St. Thomas and the Gentiles* (1938) by Mortimer J. Adler, Ph.D., associate professor of the philosophy of Law, University of Chicago.

*St. Thomas and the Greeks* (1939) by Anton C. Pegis, Ph.D., associate professor of philosophy, Fordham University.

*The Nature and Functions of Authority* (1940) by Yves Simon, Ph.D., associate professor of philosophy, University of Notre Dame.

*St. Thomas and Analogy* (1941) by the Rev. Gerald B. Phelan, Ph.D., president of the Pontifical Institute of Mediaeval Studies, University of Toronto.

*St. Thomas and the Problem of Evil* (1942) by Jacques Maritain, Ph.D., professor of philosophy, Institute of Mediaeval Studies, University of Toronto.

*Humanism and Theology* (1943) by Werner Jaeger, Ph.D., Litt.D., "university" professor, Harvard University.

*The Aquinas Lecture, 1943*

# HUMANISM
## AND
# THEOLOGY

Under the Auspices of the Aristotelian Society
of Marquette University

BY

WERNER JAEGER
*Professor at Harvard University*

MARQUETTE UNIVERSITY PRESS
MILWAUKEE
1943

First Printing, 1943
Second Printing, 1967

Library of Congress Catalog Number 43-17104



PRINTED
IN
U.S.A.

PRINTED AT THE MARQUETTE UNIVERSITY PRESS
MILWAUKEE, WISCONSIN

## THE AQUINAS LECTURES

The Aristotelian Society of Marquette University each year invites a scholar to speak on the Philosophy of St. Thomas Aquinas. These lectures have come to be called the Aquinas Lectures and are customarily delivered on the Sunday nearest March 7, the feast day of the Society's patron saint.

This year the Society has the pleasure of recording the lecture of Werner Jaeger, Ph.D., Litt.D., "university" professor at Harvard University and director of the Harvard Institute for Classical Studies.

Born at Lobberich, Germany, in 1888, Prof. Jaeger received his early education at the Gymnasium Thomaeum at Kempen in the Rhineland. In 1907 he attended the University of Marburg and thereafter the University of Berlin, whence he gained his doctorate in 1911.

In 1913 he taught at the University of Berlin and in 1914 at the University of Basel, Switzerland, where he was professor of Greek language and literature. He became full professor of classics at the University of Kiel, Germany, in 1915 and in 1921 returned to the University of Berlin as full professor of classics, holding that chair until 1936. He was also dean of the philosophy faculty during 1931-32. He came to this country in 1936 as professor of Greek at the University of Chicago and remained there until 1939, when he joined the Harvard faculty as university professor and director of the Institute for Classical Studies, which was established that year.

Prof. Jaeger visited the University of California in 1934 as Sather professor of classical literature. He gave the 1936 Gifford Lectures at the University of St. Andrews, Scotland.

He was a member of the Central Directorate of the Archaeological Institute of the German Reich until 1936 and, from 1926 to 1930, was president of the Association of Classical Scholars, Archaeologists and Ancient Historians. He is a member of the Academies of Berlin, Copenhagen, Munich, Stockholm and Bologna, of the British and American Academies, and of the Humanistic Societies at Lund and Budapest. He is, besides, an honorary fellow of the Society for Hellenic Studies in London and an honorary member of Phi Beta Kappa.

Three universities have awarded him the honorary degree of Doctor of Letters: Manchester, 1927; Cambridge, 1931, and Harvard, 1936.

Prof. Jaeger has contributed to most of the leading publications of classical scholarship, and was himself editor of *Die Antike* (1925-37) and of *Neue Philologische Untersuchungen* (1926-1936).

Among the most important of his many works are: *Entstehungsgeschichte der Metaphysik des Aristoteles* (1912); *Nemesius von Emesa* (1913); *Aristoteles* (1923, English edition 1934); *Plato im Aufbau der griechischen Bildung* (1928); *Demosthenes* (1938); and *Paideia, The Ideals of Greek Culture,* vol. I (1st edition in 1933, English edition 1939, translated into several languages; vols. II and III will be published by the Oxford University Press, N. Y., in 1943, and other volumes are in preparation). His Gifford Lectures of 1936, *Theology of the Early Greek Philosophers,* is not yet published.

He is also engaged in preparing a critical edition of the works of St. Gregory of Nyssa, the first two volumes of which were published in 1922 and 1923 under the title *Gregorii Nysseni Opera.*

To these the Aristotelian Society takes great pleasure in adding *Humanism and Theology.*

# Humanism and Theology

The problem of humanism and theology was suggested to me by the fact that the Aristotelian Society invited me, the classical humanist and student of Greek philosophy, to deliver this year's Aquinas Lecture. I appreciate that invitation as a signal honor, but to speak of St. Thomas is a little embarrassing for someone who cannot claim possession of specialized scholarship in the field of medieval philosophy. It goes without saying that this is not the first time in my life that I turned to the great Christian pupil of Aristotle, and I confess to have a profound admiration for the supreme master of medieval Christian thought. I shall try to make my contribution to your annual commemoration of him by discussing not some technical details of St. Thomas' and Aristotle's philosophy but the more general historical problem of the theocentric view of the world represented by St. Thomas and its relationship to the Greek ideal of culture and the classical tradition which is the foundation of all humanism.[1]

As everyone knows, the so-called humanists of the Renaissance who wished to revive and continue the ancient culture of Greece and Rome which they admired, thought of the Middle Ages as being exactly what the name says—and that name is their own invention—namely a barbaric period interrupting the steady growth of classical civilization. Consequently they tried to forget about the immediately preceding centuries and to go back to antiquity and the classical authors to the rediscovery of whom they made such enormous contributions that they left little to do in that respect to their more learned successors. It is of course only natural that they, in their deep admiration of classical beauty, should feel a new urge to realize that ideal in their own environment and personal style. But their opposition to the Middle Ages went farther than that. Even though most of them were not at all opposed to Christian religion, they were more of *this* world and had a new concept of human nature. When Erasmus called his human ideal *philosophia Christi*, or other humanists defined their educational aim as *sapiens et eloquens pietas,* they did not mean to say that they wanted to continue in the universities of Europe the tradition of medieval philosophy. Erasmus admired St. Thomas, but he was opposed as most of the humanists of his age to the somewhat degenerated form in which they had known "scholastic" tradition in their own time. They intended to give Christian culture a new classical form.[2] The authority of Aristotle also was affected by this turn to new ideals of learning. And even nowadays some scholars seem to think that this attitude of the humanists of the Renaissance to medieval philosophy is one of the articles of faith of all true humanism.

On the other hand, we have developed in modern historical research a feeling of historical continuity worlds apart from what the humanists of the 15th century thought true and self-evident. They would be astonished to see how "medieval" they appear to us, in some regards, and how modern the Middle Ages. Today we look no longer upon the period which built the cathedrals and created the treasures of medieval painting and sculpture as a time of barbarism, and the towering architecture of St. Thomas' philosophical system is not less imposing than the cathedrals of stone constructed by the masters of his age.[3] For a scholar such as I, who have traced back the cultural ideals of humanism to classical Greece itself[4] and have always tried to see Greek philosophy as a part of Greek culture, the special problem arises whether the philosophy of Aristotle, to which St. Thomas and the medieval philosophers turned with such a keen enthusiasm, really was a sort of extraterritorial spot on the Greek soil on which the later ambassadors of Christianity might build their residence, or whether it belonged organically to the entire development of the Greek spirit; and if so, what consequences that involves for the relationship of humanism to St. Thomas who embraced that Greek philosophical tradition.

I shall try to outline my view of the situation of humanism with regard to medieval tradition and the problem of theology[5] in particular in three parts:

1. The humanistic aspect of St. Thomas' theocentric view of the world;
2. The position and special character of his age in the historical series of revivals of classical culture to which it belongs;
3. The position of humanism with regard to the theological problem or the two basic forms of humanism.

## I

Let us turn now to the first part of our task, the humanistic aspect of the theocentric world of St. Thomas. By a theocentric view of the world I understand the view that all parts of human life and of reality at large were referred by medieval thinkers and by every faithful Christian to God as the absolute norm of perfection and the highest principle of being. The theoretical system in which this view was laid down we call theology. Theology is neither a medieval nor a Christian but a classical Greek word about which I shall speak later.[6] Perhaps the mere fact of its pre-Christian origin is a sufficient reason for not restricting our discussion to the Christian form of theology of which we think first when we apply this term and which we call more specifically "revealed" theology. The concept of theology originally meant every form of rational approach to the problem of God. The Christian philosophers used to call this "first philosophy" in the sense of Aristotle or "natural" theology as opposed to the supra-natural kind. But although Christian theology culminates in revealed or supra-natural theology, it by no means excludes the rational or natural theology of the ancient philosophers. Of course, the attitude of the different forms of Christian theology towards this problem varies greatly, but the theology of St. Thomas is characterized by putting a strong emphasis on the rational aspect of the problem which had, at his time, been placed in a surprising light by the recent discovery of Aristotle's main works hitherto unknown to the Western nations of the medieval world.[7] The first philosophy or metaphysics of Aristotle in particular was the great novelty that gave to the theological speculation of St. Albert of Cologne and St. Thomas of Aquino the decisive impulse.[8] St. Thomas, it is true, distinguished clearly between philosophy in the Greek sense of the term and theology as Christian revelation.[9] However, that did not prevent him from making full use of the unexpected ally who had appeared from the camp of the ancient Greek philosophers. The new Aristotle gave the astonished world the example of a theology worked out on the basis of pure reason with an admirable logical consistency and architectonic power. And he found the theologians of the Middle Ages prepared to appreciate this bold achievement and to learn from it for their own purpose.

The reception of Aristotle resulted in a tremendous expansion of material knowledge in every field of learning and had a profound effect on the logical methods of thought.[10] It brought about for the first time in the intellectual history of the Middle Ages a systematic construction of the universe and of man's place in it. The barriers of mere sensual experience which had kept most of the thought of the early Middle Ages within narrow bonds, with the transcendental Christian faith soaring high over these planes the while, were all of a sudden expanded into the lucid structure of the Aristotelian cosmos of *formae sub-*

*stantiales.*[11] One might describe the impression in the words of the ancient philosopher-poet Lucretius:[12]

*moenia mundi discedunt.*

The walls of the old world collapse, and it expands into clear and wide perspectives. In the hierarchy of this cosmos, what we call "things" are the materialization of the ideal forms which are the essence and constitute the reality of everything. It is these forms which we grasp in our logical concepts. With the students of St. Thomas, to whom he explained the new books of Aristotle in his lectures as his preserved commentaries on them illustrate, we climb up from step to step on the ascending scale of the "grades of human knowledge" until we finally arrive at the highest principle of the world. That is the form without matter which is "pure act" and moves the whole world and its creatures as the beloved moves the lover, i.e., it moves without being moved, through its very perfection.[13]

This was the vision which Aristotle opened up to the eyes of the new generation. Should they have refrained from following him on this way simply because they knew that the Christian religion is something different from mere intellectual vision, the *theoria* of the Greeks, and that faith is not the product of an independent effort of human reason but, as the Church taught, a gift of divine grace? They were fully aware of the profound difference of faith and reason and did not want to detract anything from the greatness of faith when they turned with such zeal to the newly discovered sources of a highly intellectualized, old and noble culture. They appreciated Aristotle's philosophy as a great achievement in itself, an achievement which seemed to place within their reach the ideal of a complete harmony between faith and reason. That harmony is itself a Greek ideal which they applied to the Christian situation. As Plato wanted to bring about in his educational system the harmony of the rational and irrational elements in human nature,[14] and as the Greeks before Plato wanted to create a harmony of body and soul by their educational system of gymnastics and music,[15] so the Christian philosophers, following them on this way, tried to bridge the gap between faith and reason. They saw them as two heterogeneous forces which naturally converged towards the same end. If they had had no faith, they would not have succeeded, they would not even have tried this synthesis. But they acted under the law of that eternal truth of St. Anselm of Canterbury: *credo ut intelligam.* And they did not necessarily agree with Tertullian's brilliant but somewhat paradoxical polemic epigram: *credo quia absurdum.* They were, in some respects, nearer the heights of classical Greek culture of the time when Aristotle had been seeking the scientific expression for his Platonic faith which had been implanted in his heart in his early youth than they were to those Christian extremists who like Tatian the

Assyrian went so far in their contempt of Greek civilization that they felt that Christianity was and should remain a strong and barbarous faith[16] and that that was what made it superior to all Hellenic culture.

Let us now try to see the attitude of St. Thomas' theology towards Greek metaphysics somewhat more from afar. Even after his time the sceptical reserve of many of his contemporaries towards the new rationalism in theology did not die out entirely. It will be good to dwell somewhat longer on this point and to approach St. Thomas' Aristotelianism from the opposite angle, in order to be able to appreciate it for what it really is—a true renaissance of the classical spirit in the middle of the 13th century. If we want to see St. Thomas in that light we must not contrast him with the later humanists of the Italian Renaissance but with another type of Christian piety less susceptible to the influence of Greek philosophy. I do not mean to compare St. Thomas' theology here with the theology of the Protestant reformers of the 16th century who were partly opposed to the Aristotelian philosophy or to the philosophical treatment of theology; most of all I do not mean to compare St. Thomas with Martin Luther who scolded Aristotle, the old pagan. Let us rather keep within the boundaries of the medieval Church. Two centuries later than St. Thomas another Thomas appeared, the famous author of the *Imitatio Christi,* a book translated into innumerable languages and of world wide circulation up to the present day. The author was inspired by a profound mystic piety. I am speaking of Thomas a Kempis. He warned the Christian reader against the dangers of intellectualism in religion when he began the second chapter of his first book with the words:[17] *"Omnis homo naturaliter scire desiderat, sed scientia sine timore Dei quid importat?"*

I listened to the message of that humble wisdom from the years of my early youth, for I was brought up, though not a member of the

Church myself, in a Catholic classical school called Gymnasium Thomaeum in the small medieval town of Kempen near the Dutch frontier of the Rhineland. It was the birthplace of Thomas a Kempis, and the statue of the saintly man above the portal of the towering castle which harbored our school looked down upon the start of my humanistic career. Later, after having studied Aristotle for many years, when I reread the *Imitatio Christi* I saw with a light shock that Thomas' words, quoted above, contained a literal allusion to the first sentence of Aristotle's *Metaphysics*. It says: "Every man has a natural desire for knowledge."[18] When Thomas a Kempis repeats these words and adds: "But what is the good of human wisdom without the fear of God?", he obviously intends to hit the pride of the scholastic philosophers of his time and their heated controversies about dogmatic questions which they carried on in their classrooms with the methods of Aristotelian dialectic. "Why bother about the *genera* and *species* of all things?" he exclaims in another passage (Chapter 3, section 2); "he to whom the eternal Word speaketh, is not troubled by the flood of human opinions. Through one Word are all things and all praise this One and it is this One that speaketh unto us."[19] That is another warning against philosophy and rational methods in theology voiced by a man whose mystic intuition leaves far behind itself the entire realm of discursive thought and easily ascends from the sensual world of the manifold to the supersensual oneness of all things.

Obviously the "natural desire of all men for knowledge" with which Aristotle starts his *Metaphysics* was the fact to which the Thomists would refer whenever religious objections in the manner of Thomas a Kempis were raised against their philosophical undertaking. From that principle Aristotle deduced step by step the concept of a supreme science or rational theology. His scholastic followers would insist that the fear of God, which is stressed by Thomas a Kempis, and their own philosophical approach were not mutually exclusive.[20] If the nature of man, so they might reply, includes as one of its essential elements the desire for knowledge, that desire has been implanted in it by the Creator. In their opinion the example of Aristotle's metaphysics showed that the inborn potentiality of and desire for knowledge, when actualized in the right manner through methodical training of the mind, leads finally to the knowledge of God as the highest grade of reality and perfection. That explains why God created human nature with the desire for knowledge, for true knowledge would lead man to Him. Thus it is not at all a sign of higher piety to neglect a faculty which was given to man for this supreme task of his education and for the true fulfillment of his destination. St. Thomas Aquinas teaches with Aristotle that everything aims naturally at its own perfection, as matter aims at its form. The very fact that human nature aims at knowledge and has a desire for it, implies that knowledge contributes to the perfection of man, and that actual knowledge is related to the mere potentiality for it, in human nature, as form is related to matter.[21]

So the concept of human nature becomes a vital problem in a discussion of the merits of philosophy and science from the theological viewpoint of St. Thomas. His Aristotelian concept of man as a rational being makes its influence felt not only in his attitude to metaphysical speculation which, as we saw, he appreciates very highly as a branch of theological studies separate from sacred theology. We encounter it also in his ethics which is built on the Aristotelian definition of human felicity as the activity of man according to the rational faculty of his soul.[22] "Nature" is a Greek concept which implies a specific mental approach to reality. Its admission includes the acceptance of a perfectly objective attitude of the observer's mind towards the world. Every theology which takes over this idea thereby admits that the rational approach to reality is of fundamental importance for its task. Thus if our analysis of St. Thomas' position is correct in stressing the fact that his system inaugurates a new and more intense evaluation of the rational aspect of human nature and of the world at large, we have anticipated, to a certain degree, the answer to our question about the relationship of humanism and the theocentric view of Thomism and medieval theology.

What then is this answer? The point of departure for every humanism must be its concept of human nature. That is a Greek heritage which St. Thomas and humanism have in common. And the rational approach of St. Thomas to reality, even the reality of God, which he shares with humanism, is a heritage of the Greeks too. Human nature and reason are the pillars of Greek culture. They both became central concepts for St. Thomas through his Aristotelianism. Consequently, we are bound to state the fact that there exists in St. Thomas, to say the least, a strong element of humanism, not only in the sense of classical tradition and the profound effect which it exercised on him, but also in the more specific sense that his thought is rationalized methodical thought because he adheres to the classical concept of human nature as that of a rational being.

## II

I have used the term "humanism" up to this point in the sense of *classical* humanism without giving it any dogmatic meaning (except for the statement that *somehow* it is concerned with human nature and with reason as the supreme force of human nature). The word "humanism" itself is not very old. It was coined by historical scholars of the 19th century who were interested in the so-called "humanists" of the 15th and 16th centuries. The latter received their name from the fact that their learned efforts to revitalize the rediscovered literature and culture of Greece and Rome centered about an ideology which was expressed in the one word *humanitas*. They took that concept from one of their greatest ancient authorities in cultural matters, Cicero. The works of that Roman orator and statesman contained many enthusiastic statements about the unique value of Greek literature and its great authors as models of human culture. In calling their culture "humanity"

Cicero did not think of philanthropy as some scholars have interpreted it, although philanthropy was duly appreciated by the Greeks and was a word invented by them. The more specific sense which Cicero gives the word *humanitas* in many passages of his works is an educational one. As the ancient grammarian Aulus Gellius (2nd century) rightly observes, the Latin *humanitas* in this sense corresponds to the Greek *paideia*.[23] Cicero understands by it the arts and letters of the Greeks, insofar as they represent the Greek ideal of man which is expressed in them. Cicero ascribes to the Greek spirit a humanizing influence; it helps man to discover his true self and thereby shape his personality. It exercises that influence because it puts before our eyes with overwhelming clarity that ideal pattern of humanity which stirs our admiration and with it one of the most powerful human instincts upon which all education and progress depends, the instinct of imitation.

When the scholars of the 15th century rediscovered most of the ancient Greek and Roman authors who had been unknown to the Middle Ages, they experienced in their own intellectual life and in their enthusiasm for the great ancient authors that wholesome effect on their personal culture which Cicero had described as *humanitas* in the Greeks. That is the reason why we find in the works of that period from which we date the beginning of modern civilization so many references to Cicero's concept of *humanitas*.[24] It is indeed the best expression for their own tendencies. But there are still other words in which the humanists tried to say how they felt about the ancients. Taking over from the Middle Ages a Christian term which originally meant something like a spiritual rebirth, *renascentia* or *renovatio,* they applied it to the revival of the arts and letters in their own time.[25] Therefore when we use nowadays the word *renaissance* to signify one individual period of history, we think in the first place of the humanists and the entire civilization of the 15th and 16th centuries; that is due mostly to Jacob Burckhardt's classical book on the culture of the Renaissance.[26]

Only gradually has modern historical research arrived at the conclusion that this period is *only* the most famous and brilliant example of a cultural rebirth which coincides with and runs parallel to a revival of classical culture. But today it no longer needs to be proved that there has been a permanent tendency of revival throughout the last millennia of Western civilization—not to speak of the East which is a problem in itself. That tendency has culminated in certain historical periods. In this sense we now speak without hesitation of the Roman civilization of Cicero's own time and of the Augustan age as a renaissance of Greek cultural ideals. Another example of which we speak too little is that of the fourth century, A.D., when a complete revival of classical Greek literature and thought took place in the Greek Christian East, and a revival of Roman literature in the Latin speaking West culminating in St. Augustine. There are still people who do not realize that what we have in both hemispheres of the late Roman empire at that time was one of the most creative civilizations which history has ever seen. The synthesis of Christian religion and classical Greek and Roman culture which it effected became classical in its turn for the following centuries of the Middle Ages, and for countless millions of people it still is. Again after the barbarous centuries of the early Middle Ages, the long and turbulent period of migration and conquest, we have a Carolingian revival of ancient Latin literature in the Occident and, contemporary and parallel to it, the Greek revival of the 9th century, the period of the famous Byzantine theologians and humanists Photius and Arethas in the Eastern Church. Without these two revivals in the East and West there would be no ancient classics left. But they kept the torch burning, and the manuscripts which they wrote are mostly the oldest witnesses which preserved to us the classical authors.

The rhythmical movement of the intellectual history of Europe reached a new climax in the age of St. Thomas. The rediscovery of the unknown works of Aristotle which we mentioned was by no means the only event that characterizes that period as a new revival of classical civilization. It was accompanied and preceded by a number of similar discoveries in the field of ancient Greek literature and science, and we must see the rebirth of Aristotelian philosophy against this broader background. The tremendous influx of classical Greek learning which Western Europe experienced during the 12th and 13th centuries came partly through the Arabs and Jews in Spain and North Africa, partly through the Arabic civilization in Sicily and Southern Italy. Another part of it stemmed from the Basilian monasteries in Southern Italy, for Calabria had a Greek population throughout the Middle Ages, and the Calabrian monasteries were a stronghold of classical Greek tradition long before the Greek scholars came over to Italy after the conquest of Constantinople by the Turks in the 15th century. The Arabs had gradually taken over the Greek learning ever since they began to conquer the Near East and Africa in the 7th century, and had developed it independently. They brought with them to Sicily and Spain the treasures of classical Greek science and philosophy in the form of Arabic translations which were translated in turn into Latin in order to make them accessible to Christian Europe. Soon the original works followed the Arabic translations, and they were translated directly from Greek into Latin. So Ptolemy's geographical and astronomical books, Galen's and Hippocrates' medical works, Nemesius' *On the Nature of Man,* Euclid's mathematical standard book, the *Elements,* and other scientific works of the Greeks appeared in the West in the 12th century.[27]

For the first time Western Europe began to participate actively in the international intellectual life of the time which had arisen in the East. It was a general rebirth of the Greek scientific tradition. The rediscovery of Aristotle in St. Thomas' time was only a partial if vitally important phase of that general movement. The theological world of St. Thomas' age, which was the leading intellectual element of Western Europe, played an outstanding part in this spiritual drama. Its main interest was naturally concentrated in Aristotle, for his philosophy offered both the Christian and the other monotheistic religions, the Mohammedans and Jews, the methods and ideas which made it possible for them to amalgamate all the rest of the scientific culture of the Greeks with their transcendental religion. St. Thomas' ardent admiration for the new Aristotle and the creative use which he makes of this discovery for his own philosophy is by far the most striking feature in the entire picture of this first awakening of

Hellenism in the Western world. Together with the revival of Greek medical, astronomical and mathematical science which accompanied it, it marked the first awakening of rationalism in Europe since the end of the ancient period. It anticipated the rationalism of the Renaissance of the 15th and 16th centuries which added Plato and the Neoplatonists, the Stoic and Epicurean philosophy and many other works of Greek science and revived the knowledge of the Greek language throughout Europe. But in some respects the rationalism of the pre-Renaissance of the time of St. Thomas was more powerful and unified in its effects on the life of that highly theological period and it laid the foundations for any further rational development, both religious and profane. Without it the Renaissance of the 15th century certainly would not have been what it was.[28]

The revival of the 12th and 13th centuries also marked a turn from the *arts* to the great *authors,* one of the main characteristics of every true classical revival. The very fact that the intellectual progress of the new age set in with and went parallel to the gradual rediscovery of a great civilization of the past made the more advanced minds of that time aware of the shallowness of the narrow channels through which the profane knowledge of the so-called liberal arts, the *trivium* and *quadrivium,* had come down to them from the classical period in a number of arid text books. A truly humanistic consciousness dawned on them of what we would call the historicity of the human spirit. The highest values of human culture naturally appeared to them as the unexpected gifts of a historical tradition of almost boundless spiritual wealth and depth. Aristotle himself and his age had seen civilization in this light. He was aware that his own philosophy and the mature scientific and moral standards of his time were the final product of a long and toilsome historical growth. St. Thomas who learnt philosophy from this ancient model felt so even more strongly, since the change of the cultural situation which had been brought about by the discovery of Aristotle and the other Greek authors was so rapid and violent.[29] It now was the most urgent task not to learn from the dogmatic wisdom of the old textbooks of the "liberal arts" but to arrive at a genuine understanding of the truly great masters of the past and to wrestle with them as Jacob wrestled with the angel of Jahwe. For the ultimate aim of this profound study of the classical tradition of philosophy was of course not to know what others had thought but to recognize the truth.[30]

The outstanding examples of this attitude are St. Thomas' commentaries, most of all those on Aristotle. They show a new concentration on understanding both the spirit and the letter of a new author who offers serious difficulties to the expert and insurmountable obstacles to the untrained average reader. When it is often said that the Renaissance was more given to the study of the authors than the Middle Ages it ought not to be overlooked that the zeal of the humanist-poets of the 15th and 16th centuries was almost entirely dedicated to the clever poetic imitation or learned quotation of the classical models. But there is nothing in that age which could be compared with the seriousness and tenacity of St. Thomas' successful attempt at understanding the works of the great philosopher to whose analysis and interpretation such a large portion of his life was devoted.[31] We do not find examples of that kind of understanding which is at once detailed and comprehensive, creative and yet entirely objective, even when we compare the centuries of the more learned and antiquarian humanism which succeeded the period of the humanist-poets of the Renaissance. The latter mostly saw the ancient world only as a background for their own self-centered and ephemerous activities and not as an object of congenial and self-effacing devotion. Only in the 19th century the medieval ideal of understanding and interpretation as an higher art was renewed in the field of classical studies. Again as in the Middle Ages it developed in connection with the enthusiastic revival of Greek philosophy which followed as an intellectual reaction the period of the so-called enlightenment of the 18th century. And from this sphere it was gradually transferred to other parts of literature—an interesting parallel which throws light on the modernity of St. Thomas' attitude towards ancient philosophy. It also deserves to be noted that he kept that interpretation of Aristotle strictly separated from his systematic theology.

Humanistic is also the determination with which he tried to go back from the Aristotle of the Arabic commentators to the true Aristotle and his endeavor to replace the older Arabic-Latin translations by new versions made directly from the Greek original. It is true, the knowledge of the Greek language which had died out at the end of the ancient period in the bilingual culture of Western

Europe, was practically lost during the Middle Ages[32] and the time of St. Thomas had to absorb the new treasures of the Greek heritage through the indirect channels of Latin commentaries and translations. Nevertheless it was a genuine renaissance of the Greek spirit. That was possible because the rational elements of Greek civilization, philosophy and science, were more easily adaptable through the medium of translation and by a mere intellectual effort than would have been Greek poetry, which they did not possess. If the individual genius of a nation is manifest only in its great poetical creations, then it is undeniable that ancient Greece in its more personal aspect was revealed only after the rediscovery of Homer and Attic tragedy in the 15th century. But St. Thomas' time was by no means one-sidedly interested in rational thought. Latin classical poetry, as Vergil's leading role in Dante's *Comedy* shows, took the place which in an historically complete picture of Greece would be claimed by Homer. Dante alone can present to us the spirit of the time in its entirety. He more than anyone else reveals to us the full humanistic meaning of St. Thomas' philosophy and the Aristotelian revival. How could one imagine the world of this first and greatest of all Italian humanists without the philosophy of St. Thomas and Aristotle which connects in Dante's poem the earthly and the celestial spheres?[33]

When the poet meets in the Inferno his beloved master, Ser Brunetto Latini, and, deeply moved by grief and sympathy, gives way to his feelings of loyalty and gratitude to him, he praises him, the fine educator and humanist, as the man who had taught him

*come l'uom' s'eterna.*

It is true, these famous words are understood by the learned interpreters of Dante's poem as meaning "how man wins eternal fame."[34] That fits the spirit of the Renaissance humanists who revived the classical passion for glory. But as a characterization of the medieval scholar Ser Brunetto, the author of *Il Tesoro,* a book whose ethical part reflects on every page the influence of Aristotle's *Nicomachean Ethics,*[35] it seems to me more appropriate to interpret this line as a hint at Aristotle's word in the *Ethics* which sums up the educational aim of his philosophy: that man should not be contented with *human* things but try to partake of *eternal* life as far as possible (ἀθανατίζειν, *s'eternar*). Aristotle is thinking of the contemplative life of the philosopher and the vision of God in which his ideal of the philosophical life reaches its climax.[36] I do not know any other description of the humanism of St. Thomas and Dante which reveals its essence with equal clarity: their ideal of human life includes the presence of the Divine.

## III

But perhaps somebody might object and say that this very attitude of Dante and St. Thomas is not humanism in the *specific* sense of the term but rather the contrary to it. Humanism, so they might say, is that modest attitude towards life which never transcends the limits of human nature. And as *they* interpret human nature, they would say that St. Thomas and Dante and all theological systems do transcend those limits because they try to enter the realm of the unknowable. There is a group of modern thinkers who have adopted the word "humanism" in this new sense of an agnostic philosophy. Without entering a more detailed discussion of their view of human nature we may briefly say that they confine knowledge to the immediate sensual experience of man's natural and social environment. So far as they have to admit the fact of the existence of religious ideas and ethical beliefs which pretend to transcend the frontiers of our material world, they take these ideas not as objective truth but as the products of a practical experience of life which has shaped its symbolic expression in the form of such ideas because it has found them helpful in making life tolerable. Such a theory does not necessarily include the dogmatic negation of religion as untrue; on the contrary, it attributes to the so-called higher values of humanity and to religious symbols some sort of "pragmatic" truth. But it does deny emphatically the possibility of that rational approach to the realm of the invisible which we call philosophy in the sense of Plato and Aristotle or of St. Thomas. Consequently, if we were to give the concept of humanism the anti-metaphysical meaning which it has for these modernists, that would decide the question of the relationship of humanism and theology in the negative.[37]

At first sight this might appear only as a struggle about words, for, as we have pointed out before, the name of humanism has been used in a different sense by most historical scholars for almost a century, before it was restricted by these modern philosophers to their theory of relativism. Thus there seems to be no reason for giving up the established and well founded terminology which identifies or connects humanism with *classical* humanism. But one who knows history might take up the defense of the new humanists and say that the so-called modest modern concept of human nature which they have adopted and which excludes man from the superhuman is in better agreement both with the humility of Christian faith and with the true spirit of classical culture. Such humanism has indeed its roots in ancient philosophical theories as has more or less every idea which we think is modern. It is a return to the ancient Greek sophists, especially Protagoras of Abdera, who lived in the time of Pericles (5th century, B.C.) He taught that man is the measurement of all things. The relativistic meaning of this doctrine is illustrated by another statement of this leading sophist with which he began his work *On the Gods:* "Regarding the gods I have no way of knowing whether they exist or whether they do not."[38]

Protagoras does not deny their existence dogmatically but leaves it to our personal "will to believe," to speak with William James, whether we want to accept it or not. Now it is a well known fact that the Greek sophists were the founders of the theory of an education and were the first to formulate the idea of a culture which became very important in the history of classical and modern humanism. They were in the first place not philosophers but educators. Thus if the modern philosophers who called themselves humanists were more interested in the history of mankind than they usually are, they might say that it is a fact of profound significance that the ideal of culture arose at the same historical moment and in the same circle that created the relativistic doctrine: man is the measurement of all things. For does that not prove that all our theorizing about culture and education and the ideal of human civilization *is* a product of that wise self-restriction of sophistic philosophy which told man to refrain from speculating about the inscrutable and to concentrate on his own perfection? The Greeks called this cultural effort *paideia.*[39] Paideia as we have seen was the historical root of what Cicero praised as the *humanitas* of the Greeks. Cicero himself though he had a deeply religious nature, was a sceptic with regard to the transcendental philosophy of his time and the metaphysical use of reason, as he often states in his philosophical works.[40] Shall we draw from this coincidence the inference that a fundamental lack of certainty about what St. Thomas calls *aeterna veritas* is the very root of all humanism, not only that of the modern relativism which claims that title but also its classical prototype, the humanism of ancient Greece and Rome? It then would follow that the word humanistic means *anthropocentric* in a sense which excludes a *theocentric* view of the world.

There are many scholars in our days who believe that humanism is identical with this anthropocentric view. Therefore they look upon the sophists and their contemporaries and companions, the ancient teachers of rhetoric like Gorgias and Isocrates and the later Quintilian, as the true fathers of humanism. No one can deny that many humanists in modern times resemble that pattern. I am speaking of those whose ideal of education and culture is of a merely formalistic nature.[41] From a Thomist point of view Jacques Maritain pointed out a few years ago in his book *Humanisme Intégral* (Paris, 1936) that if this be humanism, a man of his convictions must either abandon humanism entirely or redefine it. He has proposed an interpretation which allows him to take the word in a sense which includes the great transcendental tradition of Western civilization.[42] I, on my part, have not approached humanism here and elsewhere from the side of systematic philosophy, but from the historical point of view. I have traced it back to the spiritual sources of all humanism in the classical world. We have seen before that it goes back to the Greek ideal of human culture. But that ideal appears in the intellectual history of Greece in more than one form. We find the stratification and the antinomies of our modern cultural consciousness reflected in the most striking manner in the succession and mutual struggle of the cultural ideals of ancient Greece. Against the paideia of the sophists and rhetoricians from which we have derived the relativistic kind of modern humanism there arose the paideia of Socrates, Plato and Aristotle. To them we must turn now, in order to contrast them with their famous predecessors.[43]

In the light of Plato's Socratic dialogues the humanism of the sophists appears not at all as the climax but as a symbol of the decline of Greek civilization. They introduced a period of social and intellectual disintegration. Of course the sophists were not alone responsible for the increasing decay of ethical and religious tradition. They were only the heirs who liquidated the remaining substance of a great past. The religious foundations of earlier Greek life had been crumbling gradually during the 5th century.[44] We can pursue the barometric curve of this intellectual process in the works of the three great masters of Attic tragedy, Aeschylus, Sophocles, and Euripides. At the beginning of the 5th century, B.C., we have the founder of tragedy, the prophetic Aeschylus, whose mind is deeply rooted in the religious tradition of his people. He is like a wrestler of gigantic strength. That strength is due to his unshakable confidence in the divine wisdom that governs the life of man in spite of its tragic nature which stirs the poet's human sympathy and fear. Sophocles, to my mind the greatest artist of the three, has accomplished in his work a perfect balance of the human and the divine aspects of life. He does not question the god-sent character of evil, but he has neither the power nor the desire of Aeschylus to struggle with the problem of God for its own sake. He silently bows to the inaccessible majesty of the superhuman but he turns with all his intensity towards the human side of the picture. His art is centered around the suffering and the tragic greatness of his hero, man. The third of the classical tragedians of Athens, Euripides, is an artist of tremendous gifts, but this world, entirely humanized and relativistic, lacks an absolute center. He is a sceptic, the true contemporary of Protagoras. The historian of this age, Thucydides, tells the story of the Peloponnesian war as the collapse not only of Athens' power and empire but also of Greek society, faith and morality. He shows the naturalism of his time at work in real life. And against this background we must see the sophists with their desperate idea of human culture which makes man the measurement of all things.

When Socrates, Plato and Aristotle set out on their way to reconstruct human life they were aware of the weakness of their age, but nevertheless they felt that they could bring about a solution only if they started on the same basis to which the sophistic enlightenment had transferred the problem, the basis of rational thought. In other words, they had to attack at the point of strongest resistance. Man could not return in that period of intellectual development to the mythological age. But the human culture of the "primitive" age had one great advantage over the centrifugal thought of the enlightened times of the sophists: the life of man was centered around the belief in that which is higher than man. When Plato and Aristotle, following in Socrates' footsteps, reestablished the certainty of God as the supreme principle of the natural and social world they did not mean to return to the mythological age, but they wanted to reveal the indestructible kernel of reality which religion in its mythical stage had symbolized in mythical form. Therefore they now approached that reality which religion called *theos* by means of reason, or as the Greek language says *logos.* The result of this intellectual effort is called *theologia.* The man who coined the word and established the new concept as the center of all philosophical thought was Plato.[45] St. Augustine rightly praises him as the true father of theology and Meister Eckhart calls him "the great theologian" (*"Plato, der grosse pfaffe."*[46]) It was the people of the Greeks, the founders of philosophy and science, who contributed to the intellectual life of mankind this new form of rational approach to the superhuman world. Wherever we find theology in this sense of the term it is religious life in Hellenized form.[47] Aristotle inherited it from Plato. He called his first philosophy "theology" for it is the part of philosophy which transcends the physical world.[48] Only later generations of the Aristotelian school called it "metaphysics."

Even from the little we have said it is clear that, if we really want to do justice to Plato's new conception of philosophy, his turn to the divine center of things, we must not see it as an isolated phenomenon in the history of Greek philosophy but in the closest connection with the entire development of the Greek mind and the organic changes of its social structure. Plato himself saw clearly his life work as a philosophical reconstruction of that basic social scheme of Greek life. Let us see his theological venture, in order to make this evident, against the background of the religious and social structure of early Greek life, as it is reflected in the earliest Greek poets. Homer and Hesiod were in a way also the fathers of Greek theology,[49] but it was theology only in a restricted sense. Aristotle distinguishes these early mythical theologians from his own rational theology. In Homer's all embracing picture of the world man occupies the foreground and in that sense his world is an anthropocentric one. But insofar as the gods, the rulers of this world, are always present and determine man's destiny, the epic world must be called theocentric. The gods equally determine human virtue (areté), and the true hero is called by Homer godlike, i.e., he imitates the divine pattern, however imperfect that pattern may appear from the viewpoint of a more advanced consciousness. The development of the religious ideas of the Greeks takes its departure from Homer. Hesiod, the second great epic poet, differs from Homer in that he is a tangible historical individuality. He separates the divine element of the Homeric epos from the human and entirely concentrates on the problem of the divine. His *Theogony* is the first Greek system of the gods and in that sense is a predecessor of rational theology, even though his source is still mythical tradition. His *Theogony* became the form which many successive generations used for the expression of their mythical or allegorical speculation on the nature of the gods. The need for this kind of speculation in that period is indicative of the increasing trend towards rational theology.

But the purely rational approach to the problem came from another corner of the Greek world. It came from the first philosophers who investigated the principles of nature. Aristotle calls them the physicists and contrasts them with the mythical theologians who preceded them. The 19th century has praised them as the first scientists because they tried to explain the phenomena of the material world through a rational system of natural causality. Nevertheless they ascribed to their physical principle a divine rank and nature, and St. Augustine names them first in his series of Greek philosophical theologians.[50] When later theologians used with regard to their immaterial god predicates such as boundless, eternal, all governing and all encompassing, they were not always aware of the fact that it was the so-called pre-Socratic natural philosophers who established these categories in order to describe their material principle as the divine source of life and reality. It was they who demolished the anthropomorphism of the mythical gods of the Greek tradition, and their arguments against these unworthy and imperfect gods were taken over and applied to the problem of God by Plato and by the fathers of the Christian Church in their polemic against the pagan gods. It was the pre-Socratics who partly stressed the oneness of God, although they thought of him as a principle immanent in nature. Even Anaxagoras, who said God was an infinite being and pure mind, still visualized him as a material principle.[51]

This speculative movement with its bold rational approach to the highest problem flourished in the 6th and 5th century, B.C. It came to a standstill when the sophists turned their backs to all speculation and in profound scepticism concentrated on the practical task of human education as we have pointed out before. They pretended to be teachers of civic virtue and nothing else. Instead of inquiring into the nature of the divine things, they restricted themselves to the sphere of man and to a social science without metaphysical background. But this modest way out of the desperate situation was blocked by Socrates with his famous questions. He opposed to the scepticism of the sophists in theoretical matters his practical scepticism and proved to them that there is no escape from disbelief in reason into the practical sphere of education, since true education involves more than mere methods for the training of the mind. It requires an aim towards which human action should be directed and a certainty about the good which it strives to attain. The statement of Protagoras that man himself is that measurement of all things is, from this viewpoint, only the declaration of bankruptcy of human culture.[52]

Thus Socrates set out on his tireless and lifelong search for the measurement without which education and human culture in the deeper sense cannot exist. His method was called by Plato dialectic. We cannot go here into a detailed description of that logical analysis of the conscious or subconscious foundations of human life and action. Socrates discovered the soul and explored the structure and the laws of this cosmos within man. Starting from the existence of human desires Socrates ascends to the distinction of the individually desired and the absolutely desirable which he calls "good itself." Plato, his great disciple, who portrayed his master's way in his Socrates dialogues carried on his work along this line of investigation along which Socrates had led him. His pedagogical aim in his books is to show the reader who is able to follow that this line which starts with the practical question of human education and virtue leads up, when pursued in the truly Socratic way, to the divine principle of the intelligible world which Plato calls "the unconditioned."[53] In his last work, the *Laws,* where the philosopher appears as the legislator of a new human society founded on the unshakable rock of truth, we read a word which throws a bar of light back to the beginning of Socrates' strenuous path and over Plato's entire work: God is the measurement of all things.[54] The word of Protagoras that man is the measurement is reversed and changed into its contrary. The true paideia, be it education or legislation, is founded on God as the supreme norm. It is—to speak with Plato's *Republic*—"conversion" from the world of sensual self-deception to the world of the one true being which is the absolute good and the one desirable.[55] Or in the words of Plato's *Theaetetus:* true human virtue is assimilation to God.[56]

The historical development of the Greek mind seems to move in a circle, for Plato has arrived again at the same point at which the Greek way had started. The world of Plato like that of Homer may be described as at once anthropocentric and theocentric. Man and human life are in the foreground of Socrates' and Plato's thought and in that sense it is anthropocentric; but God is in the center of that human world. In spite of this analogy with Homer the relation of man to the superhuman in Plato's philosophy is no longer the Homeric one. It is based on the intrinsic experience of the soul and its forces, most of all on the force of reason which is the golden link that connects the philosopher with God.[57] Thus the circle of which we spoke is not a real circle after all, but the development resembles a spiral which ascends and thereby arrives at a higher point perpendicularly above its point of departure. The insight into the nature of this development of the philosophical mind of the Greeks is enlightening in the highest degree. For the return of the human mind to its point of departure and the new synthesis of all the elements which had emancipated themselves from their original unity during the earlier stages of that process seems to indicate an inherent structural law of the mind which requires God as the center of its world, the cosmos both without and within.

But from the viewpoint of our question, the relation of humanism and theology, the result of our analysis is of particular interest. As we have seen, theology is conceived here for the first time in a sense comparable to that which we find in the philosophy of Aristotle and St. Thomas. The philosophical religion of the spirit which Plato calls "theology" was born, as we have shown, directly out of the crisis of the Greek cultural ideal. It was the reversal of the humanistic ideal of the sophists, but at the same time it must be called its logical product. Theology was intended from its very beginning to transcend humanism but at the same time it was the true fulfillment of the task which humanism had formulated. Plato presented his new *paideia* not in the form of an abstract system of metaphysics but as the graphic picture of an ideal state in his *Republic,* and later again in his *Laws.* Thus he gives the science of the highest principle its proper setting, for this way of ascending to it brings it home to the philosophical reader that it is at once the constructive principle of human society and of the life of the individual. But the ideal state in which it would be possible to subordinate everything to the divine rule of that principle transcends, as Plato sets forth, all states on earth in the same manner as Plato's theocentric *paideia* transcends all that is called human education in his day and not only in *his* day.[58] The social architecture which Plato describes as the ideal state is entirely devoted to the education and guidance of man and insofar resembles more the Church than the traditional Greek city state. When we pursue the idea of education in the Greek and Platonic way into its logical consequences, we arrive indeed at a concept of an ideal community such as this and an educational structure founded on God as the absolute measurement of all things.[59] It is therefore not by chance that Plato's philosophy of *paideia* which tries to correct the shortcomings of sophistic humanism, is the origin of all rational theology.

---

It is not my intention nor would it be possible within the limits of a single lecture to expand this historical view beyond the times to which the problem of humanism goes back in the last analysis, the period of the Greek sophists and Plato. I wanted to direct your attention to these origins of the cultural ideals of the Western world. We have coordinated in one field of vision and contrasted with each other the two basic forms of Greek *paideia:* that of sophistic and rhetoric, represented by Protagoras, and that of the Platonic Socrates. It would of course be of great interest from our point of view to pursue the theology created by Plato through the subsequent phases of the history of Greek philosophy. Speaking to an audience so familiar with Aristotelian and Thomist theology I need not dwell on the next and most important stage of that development, the emancipation of Aristotle's theology from the Platonic school. Aristotle followed a different method and adopted a new concept of knowledge and reality. But he agrees with his master Plato in that he conceives the first philosophy which transgresses the limits of the sensual world as essentially theology.[60] Even the Stoics and Epicureans during the Hellenistic centuries who maintained against Plato and Aristotle the materialistic concept of reality of the earlier natural philosophers incorporated in their systems a theology. But since it was unable to satisfy the demands of the Greek mind in the long run, the Christian centuries saw a powerful revival of the philosophical movement inaugurated by Plato and Aristotle. Thus we find at the end of the ancient period the theocentric philosophy of the Neoplatonists in a dominant position throughout the Greek and Roman world.

This was the intellectual situation into which Christianity entered when it emerged from the catacombs after the times of persecution and triumphantly asserted its spiritual system. It would be saying too much if one were to state that as a consequence of the philosophical thought of the Greeks the popular religion of the ancient world no longer existed at the time when the Christian missionaries appeared. But the Christian authors who had to defend their faith against the official protectors of the dwindling public cults and against the mythical deities of classical poetry joined the Greek philosophers in their attack on these two forms of traditional religion. Even though they were no longer very powerful in themselves, they were strongly supported by the political system of the Roman Empire and by the literary heritage of the classical period. Following the Roman philosopher Varro, St. Augustine opposes to the mythological and political theology of the tradition the natural theology of the philosophers and accepts it as a common basis for this fight.[61] He esteems most highly Plato, the father of theology. In order to become the universal or Catholic religion, Christianity took over the rational form of theology and dogma from Greek philosophy.[62] It seems to me idle to ask whether the faith of the fishermen of Galilee should not have preserved the original and simple form which it had in the Sermon of the Mount and resisted all contact with the Greek spirit. In that form it could not have penetrated and conquered the civilized world.

The reception of the philosophical theology of the Greeks into the Church, so far as it was commensurable with Christianity, and the development of a Christian theology and dogma did not serve only apologetic purposes. The Greek mind was either not able to adapt the Christian faith in another way or at least this was the specifically Hellenic way of adapting it to their culture. Nothing is so characteristic of the Greeks, says St. Gregory of Nyssa, one of the outstanding Christian Platonists of the 4th century, as the belief that the essence of religion lies in the dogma.[63]

He sees clearly the danger of overrating this aspect and neglecting what he calls the real strength of Christianity: the mysteries of the faith and the venerable traditions of the Church. The three elements ought to be kept in a perfect balance. Beyond the general intellectual affinity between Christian dogmatic thought and Greek philosophical theology there was also a deeper kinship of their spirit. It was so close that, as St. Augustine in his *Confessions* tells us, he received the first impulse to his conversion from reading not the Scriptures but a book in which Cicero had reproduced a platonizing work of the young Aristotle, the *Exhortation to Philosophy.*[64] There were many who came to Christianity in this way.

We have discussed here the problem of theology from the humanistic viewpoint and as a basic element of classical humanism; therefore the turn of ancient Greek theology to Christian theology cannot be included here: it is a great problem in itself.[65] But the original connection between theology and the cultural idea *(paideia)* was preserved in the Christian times. It would be a mistake to think that they were ever divorced from each other and that, when theology was Christianized, *paideia* was dismissed. The history of Christian literature can be written from this point of view, i.e., as a history of the gradual realization of the idea of a Christian civilization in all its essential aspects. Theology is throughout conceived by the Christian writers as the principle of a new culture and not as a shapeless religious irrationalism. The *Acts of the Apostles* represent St. Paul as the first to acknowledge the great historical task of a synthesis of ancient culture and the Christian spirit. Standing on the august ground of the Athenian Areopagus, he tells the philosophers of Hellas who used to have their discussions there in the very center of the ancient world, that he has come in order to reveal to them the unknown God whom they had anticipated and to whom they had erected an altar. He refers to the Greek poet who had said: "We are also of divine offspring."[66] He could have quoted Plato who calls man a celestial plant. In the apocryphal *Acts of Philip, the Apostle*, a later Christian book whose author sometimes tries to vary the situations occurring in the work of his canonical predecessor, the Apostle Philip comes to Athens and speaks to the same audience, the philosophers of Greece. He tells them that Christ has come to bring the world a new culture (he says *paideia*) in order to fulfill and supersede the old culture which the audience represents.[67] The unknown author of Pseudo-Justin's book *Oratio ad gentiles* speaks of the Christian doctrine as the true *paideia*,[68] another derives it from the concept of *humanitas* ( ἀνθρωπίνη φύσις ) itself.[69]

The creation of that new Christian culture culminated in the systems of the two greatest Christian thinkers, St. Augustine and St. Thomas. They blended the two outstanding manifestations of a theocentric humanism in classical antiquity, Platonism and Aristotelianism, with the Christian faith. For whatever be the difference between Christian and ancient philosophy, they both agreed on the question which Aristotle raises at the beginning of his *Metaphysics* where he asks whether the idea of such a knowledge of the superhuman is not beyond human nature.[70] Some of the old Greek poets seem to think so, he says, and they attribute that knowledge to God alone. But with his master Plato Aristotle refused to be a Greek in that sense and proclaimed an idea of man which includes the Divine and shows the way how mortal man may participate in eternal life.[71]

## NOTES

1. That the relationship of humanism to classical antiquity is not accidental but essential to it, is an assumption that underlies the following discussion. It will be treated below in greater detail. With regard to the relation of humanism to Greece I refer to my work, *Paideia, The Ideals of Greek Culture,* vols. I-III (Oxford University Press, New York, 1939-1943). For another concept of humanism which does not attribute to classical culture a central position in it, see R. B. Perry in *The Meaning of the Humanities,* Five Essays, etc. (Princeton University Press, 1938) with the review of E. K. Rand, Philosophical Review, vol. 49 (1940) p. 672.

2. About Erasmus' humanism which he called *philosophia Christi*, see his programmatic words in his *Enchiridion militis christiani* (ed. Clericus tom. V, p. 2 f.; Desiderius Erasmus Roterodamus Ausgewaehlte Werke ed. Holborn, Munich 1933, p. 5). This new humanism was a new form of Christian theology with the emphasis on education rather than dogma. Erasmus opposed to the theology of the medieval *Summae* and *Sententiae* the simple evangelical doctrine of Christ which is accessible to everyone and not only to abstract minds trained in the methods of scholastic logic. The polemic against the predominance of scholastic theology in the universities of his age pervades all of Erasmus' theological writings; it can not be separated from the positive religious and theologi-

cal aims of his humanism. Cf. the *Praefatio* to his edition of the New Testament and the *Paraclesis* (ed. Clericus, tom. VI, p. 2 f.; Holborn, p. 139 f.) and again *Methodus* p. 156 Holb. and *Ratio seu compendium verae theologiae* (ed. Clericus tom. V, p. 75 f., Holborn, p. 177 f.), especially p. 185 f. Holb. But this book also shows that Erasmus' opposition to philosophical theology did not amount to a radical negation of its value. He only wanted to keep it within certain limits. The educational ideal of *sapiens et eloquens pietas* which was accepted by many humanists of the sixteenth century shows clearly their intention of bringing about a synthesis of the two opposite branches of ancient culture, philosophy and rhetoric, on the basis of Christian religion.

The relationship of the humanists of the early Renaissance in the fifteenth century to the religious problem has been scrutinized several times during the last few decades, but its investigation still remains a desideratum to be fulfilled in a more comprehensive style. These studies have emphasized the Christian but anti-scholastic character of early humanism, see T. Joachimsen, Historische Zeitschrift vol. 121 (1920) p. 189-233: *Aus der Entwicklung des italienischen Humanismus* and the literature on this subject which he surveys. In Italy Marsilius Ficinus and the circle of the Platonic Academy in Florence were the center of a philosophical and theological humanism. Even though there were many pagan minds among the poet-humanists of the Renaissance, the leading figures who have determined the history of humanism as a cultural ideal are distinguished by their enthusiasm for Christianity as the greatest educational force in the development of mankind. But Platonism and Stoicism played a greater part in the theological discussions of the humanists since the Renaissance than Aristotle.

3. For the revaluation of the Middle Ages at large it may suffice to refer to a few books of more general scope which are easily available to the English speaking reader: E. K. Rand, *Founders of the Middle Ages,* (Cambridge, 1928), C. H. Haskins, *The Renaissance of the Twelfth Century,* (Cambridge, 1927), H. O. Taylor, *The Medieval Mind,* (1st ed. London, 1911), K. Vossler, *Medieval Culture,* (2 vols., New York, 1930), M. L. W. Laistner, *Thought and Letters in Western Europe* A.D. 500-900, (New York, 1931). For the history of medieval philosophy see Note 10.

4. See my work *Paideia* quoted in Note 1 and my *Humanistische Reden und Vortraege* (Berlin, 1937), especially the lectures on "Humanismus als Tradition und Erlebnis" p. 18, "Antike und Humanismus" p. 110, "Kulturidee und Griechentum" p. 125.

5. Theology is not treated in this lecture in all its historical aspects, as is obvious from the following specification of the subject matter. It deals with the theology of St. Thomas and more specifically with the natural theology of the Greek thinkers and its influence on Christian medieval thought.

6. See p. 45-46 and footnote 45.

7. About the gradual rediscovery of Aristotle's works during the Middle Ages see the older book of M. Jourdain, *Recherches critiques sur l'age et l'origine des traductions latines d'Aristote* etc. (Paris 1819, 2nd ed. 1843) and now the standard works of M. DeWulf, *Histoire de la philosophie médiévale,* vol. II (6th ed.) p. 25 f. (by A. Pelzer) and M. Grabmann, *Geschichte der scholastischen Methode,* vol. II. To them must be added some more special studies about the medieval Latin translations of Aristotle by M. Grabmann, C. H. Haskins, A. Pelzer, F. Pelster, C. Marchesi and others with the titles of which I do not wish to encumber this note. The Union Académique Internationale has started after the first World War the monumental work of a complete critical edition of the medieval Latin translations of Aristotle. The present author had the privilege of cooperating with that learned committee for many years. The Medieval Academy of America embarked on the parallel plan of editing the commentaries of Averroes on Aristotle; see H. A. Wolfson, *Speculum,* vol. VI (1931) p. 412.

8. About the medieval Latin translations of Aristotle's *Metaphysics* made directly from the Greek original, see F. Pelster, *Die griechisch-lateinischen Metaphysikuebersetzungen des Mittelalters* (Muenster, 1923). The Greco-Latin versions were preceded by other Latin versions made from Arabic translations.

9. See S. Thomae Aquinatis *Summa contra gentiles* (ed. Leonina, tom. XIII, Romae, 1918) I, cap. 3 and 4 pp. 7 and 11 on *duplex veritas* and II, cap. 4; p. 278: Quod aliter considerat de creaturis philosophus et theologus.

10. About the influence of Aristotle's newly discovered works on the philosophical method of medieval Christian thought, see M. Grabmann, *Geschichte der scholastischen Methode,* vol. II (Freiburg, 1911) p. 64. É. Gilson, *L'esprit de la philosophie médiévale* (2 vols., Paris, Vrin, 1932), *Reason and Revelation in the Middle Ages* (New York, Scribners, 1939), *Christianity and Philosophy* (New York, Sheed and Ward, 1939).

11. Speaking more precisely the concept of *formae substantiales* was introduced by St. Thomas. It signifies the Aristotelian form, so far as it is the being of the first category (*esse substantiale*), which determines the *materia prima,* and not the being of the following categories (quality, quantity, relation, etc.) which determine the individual substance consisting of matter and form.

12. Lucretius, *De rerum natura,* III, 16-17.

13. S. Thomae Aquinatis, *Commentaria in XII libros Metaphysicorum Aristotelis* (Cathala ed., Marietti, Turin, 1935) XII, lect. VII, #252 f.

14. Plato, *Republic* III, 549 b.

15. Plato, *Republic* III, 412 a.

16. Tatianus, *Contra Graecos* c. 29 f., c. 35. He contrasts the Old Testament which the calls the "dogmata of the barbarians" with the Hellenic *paideia* and decides against the latter. It hardly needs to be pointed out that the attitude of the Fathers of the Church was very different from that of Tatian, as a rule. His elaborate style is not in agreement with his antipathy to Greek culture. His language shows the strong influence of Greek rhetoric in every line and proves that his practice was not quite as uncompromising as his theory. His love of the extreme drove him later to heresy.

17. Thomae Hemerken a Kempis, *Opera* (ed. M. J. Pohl, Freiburg, 1904), vol. II, p. 7. The author of this only critical edition was the Master of the Classical school at Kempen, the Gymnasium Thomaeum.

18. The Latin translation of the *Metaphysics* which St. Thomas used was made on his own instigation by Wilhelm of Moerbeke, the Flemish monk and later Archbishop of Corinth. The exact words of this translation are, "*Omnes homines natura scire desiderant.*"

19. Thomae Hemerken a Kempis, *Opera* (ed. Pohl) vol. II, p. 9.

20. After finishing the manuscript of this lecture I received through the kindness of the author, Leopoldo Zea, *Superbus Philosophus* (reprint from the volume *Trabajos de Historia Filosofica,*

*Literaria y Artistica del Christianismo y la Edad Media,* (El Colégio de México, 1942) who quotes the *Imitatio Christi* as a motto of his study. His essay is concerned with the value of ancient philosophy, seen from the Christian viewpoint. He identifies Christianity with the ideal of *humilitas* which Thomas a Kempis contrasts with the spirit of *philosophia* and "*superbia.*" From the viewpoint of St. Thomas Aquinas, Christianity and philosophy are not mutually exclusive. It is interesting for us, in an analysis of the humanistic element in medieval philosophy, to observe this difference.

21. S. Thomae Aquinatis *in lib. I Metaph. Arist.,* (Marietti ed.) lect. I, #2. A second reason for the natural desire of man for knowledge is, according to St. Thomas, that everything has the natural desire to operate in its proper way; proper to man in this sense is the operation of the intellect, since it distinguishes man from the other animals (lect. I, #3). The third reason is that everything wants to be connected with its principle. Therefore man wants to be connected with the separate substance which is the principle of the human intellect, because it shows the intellect in its perfection whereas the human intellect is imperfect. This makes the fulfillment of the human desire for knowledge imperative for the felicity of man (lect. I, #4). The same argument is used by Dante, *Convivio,* IV, XII, 14.

22. S. Thomae *Expositio in X libros Ethicorum Aristotelis ad Nicomachum* (Pirotta ed., Marietti, Turin, 1934) I, lect. X, #119-129. See also the interpretation of the human desire for knowledge as the desire for felicity in Thomas' commentary on the *Metaphysics* quoted at the end of Note 21. Concerning the relation of St. Thomas' philosophical theory of human action and beatitude to his theology see A. D. Sertillanges, S. Thomas d'Aquin (Paris, 1910) vol. II p. 302. It goes without saying that St. Thomas modified Aristotle's conception of human beatitude not a little, as is sagaciously pointed out by G. deBroglie in his careful analysis of St. Thomas' theory entitled "Autour de la notion thomiste de la béatitude" in *Archives de Philosophie,* vol. III, cahier 2: Études sur saint Thomas (Paris 1925) p. 55-96.

23. The lexicographic material for the word *humanitas* in Cicero was collected by M. Schneidewin, *Die antike Humanitaet* (Berlin 1897) p. 31-40, especially p. 37 f. See also R. Reitzenstein, *Werden und Wesen der Humanitaet in Altertum* (Strassburg, 1907), who traces the Ciceronian concept of *humanitas* back to the Scipionic circle in Rome, and the article *humanitas* by I. Heinemann in Pauly-Wissowa, *Realencyclopaedie der klassischen Altertumswissenschaft,* Suppl. V, p. 282. About the two different meanings of *humanitas, philanthropia* and *paideia,* see the Roman grammarian of the second century A.D., Aulus Gellius, *Noctes Atticae* XIII, 17.

24. The material for the concept of *humanitas* in the quattrocento humanists was collected on my instigation by Maria Meyer-Schadewaldt, but unfortunately her work was never finished.

25. F. Burdach, *Reformation Renaissance Humanismus* (Berlin, 1926) p. 1 f. has traced the origin of such words as *renascentia, renovatio,* etc. in medieval literature.

26. Jacob Burckhardt, *The Civilization of the Renaissance in Italy* (London, 1937).

27. See C. H. Haskins, *The Renaissance of the Twelfth Century* (Cambridge, 1927) p. 303 f. For a survey see G. G. Walsh, S.J., *Medieval Humanism* (New York, 1942).

28. About the first rationalism of the 12th and 13th centuries see É. Gilson, *Études de philosophie médiévale* (Strasbourg, 1921).

29. The medieval system of *artes liberales* did not, of course, cease to exist after the rediscovery of Aristotle, Euclid, Ptolemy, Hippocrates and Galen. But the interest of scholars naturally turned more and more towards the study of these great *auctores.* Sometimes modern historical scholars and classicists who were pursuing the humanistic tradition through the Middle Ages have tried to find it too exclusively in the tradition of the *artes liberales.* Nothing would be more wrong than to underrate the historical importance of that tradition for medieval humanism, but the liberal arts represented

the ancient *paideia* in its latest and thinnest form, more the skeleton to which it had been reduced for paedagogical purposes than its true self. The turn from the *artes* to the *auctores* themselves was a return to the *paideia* of the Greeks in the form which it had in its best times when it still was represented by and embodied in the great authors. In my evaluation of the humanism of St. Thomas I agree with Étienne Gilson, *Saint Thomas d'Aquin* (Paris, 1925) p. 3 f. The humanistic character of St. Thomas' attitude towards man and human culture was stressed also by M. Grabmann, *Die Kulturphilosophie des hl. Thomas von Aquin* (Augsburg, 1925) p. 58 f. While working on this lecture I received as a gift of the author, Rodolfo Mondolfo, a prominent scholar in the field of the history of ancient philosophy formerly of Bologna (Italy), now at the University of Córdoba (Argentina), his collected essays *En los orígenes de la filosofía de la cultura* (Buenos Aires, 1942). In his essay on the origin and meaning of the humanistic concept of culture, the author who pays special attention to the Renaissance humanists and their concept of the *dignitas* of man refers on p. 140 f. to St. Thomas as the outstanding medieval representative of an idea of man which emphasizes his capacity of *agere et facere* in the Aristotelian sense, and thereby anticipates to a considerable degree the idea of the Renaissance humanists of human dignity. About St. Thomas' (and Aristotle's) relationship to intellectual tradition and their concept of intellectual progress see S. Thomae *in lib. II Metaph. Arist.* (Marietti ed.) lect. 1, #287-288.

30. See S. Thomae *Expositio in libros Aristotelis de caelo et mundo* (ed. Leonina tom. III) I, lect. XXII, sect. 8; p. 91.

31. With this form of interpretation St. Thomas stands in the continuity of a great tradition of "exegetes" of Aristotle which goes back over the Arabian commentators of the Middle Ages to the long series of ancient interpreters of Aristotle's works. They are now completely edited, so far as the ancient period is concerned, in the monumental publication of the Academy in Berlin in the *Commentaria in Aristotelem Graeca* in 28 volumes. The work of commenting was started however much earlier than this series begins, by the immediate pupils of Aristotle himself who realized that the works of their master needed careful interpretation. A considerable number of fragments of their own exegesis of Aristotle is preserved by the later ancient commentators. Theophrastus and the other pupils of Aristotle were also the first in the history of philosophy to call themselves "scholastics" in an honorable sense, i.e. men who are enjoying leisure for their studies; see Theophrastus in his letter to the Peripatetic scholar Phanias in Diog. L. V. 37, where he calls himself a scholastic, and the Peripatetic Clearchus quoted by Josephus *c. Apionem* lib. I, 181. Clearchus in one of his dialogues introduced the master of the Peripatetic school as the main figure; there Aristotle

spoke of "himself and the other scholastics" i.e. the members of his school.

On the other hand, it deserves to be noted that St. Thomas in spite of his profound devotion to the "Philosophus," as he calls Aristotle, is in many respects less given to the cult of authority than the majority of the Renaissance humanists who knew and quoted more numerous classical authors than he did, but by no means always better ones. Very often to them an "authority" is simply what is Greek or Latin. St. Thomas remains throughout the discerning philosophical mind who uses his own judgment. He even develops a complete theory about the critical use of *auctoritates* which seemed to him to be the weakest form of argument, see the article of M. Riquet, "Saint Thomas d'Aquin et les 'auctoritates' en philosophie" in *Archives de Philosophie* vol. III cahier 2: Études sur saint Thomas (Paris, 1925) p. 117-155. The essay presents an abundant material of well chosen examples on this subject together with their critical evaluation.

32. On the study of Greek in the occident during the Middle Ages see M. L. W. Laistner, *Thought and Letters in Western Europe A.D. 500-900* (New York, 1931) p. 191 f.

33. See the episodes of the *Divina Commedia* where St. Thomas is glorified and makes several important speeches (Paradiso, Canto X-XIV). Aristotle's philosophy underlies Dante's poem and thought throughout as a whole and in innumerable details.

That was only natural at that time for a poet of the strong classical and philosophical interest of Dante. É. Gilson, "Dante et la philosophie" (in *Études de philosophie médiévale,* vol. XXVIII, Paris, 1939) p. 219 n. 1 speaks of the "omniprésence de l' Éthique à Nicomaque chez Dante." See also p. 145-147 about Aristotle as the "Emperor and Pope" of Dante in the field of moral philosophy. For the layman who wants to convince himself of Aristotle's position in Dante's world, it might be advisable to read Dante's *Convivio* with its numerous quotations from Aristotle on almost every page. They show that Dante lived entirely in Aristotle's work. See besides the famous but more impersonal praise of Aristotle as "il maestro di color che sanno" (Inferno, Canto IV, 131) the words *Convivio* I, IX, 9 where Dante speaks of "my master Aristotle in the first book of his *Ethics*" and the passage Inferno, Canto XI, 80 where Virgil speaks to Dante of Aristotle's *Ethics* as "la tua Etica," and Inferno, Canto XI,, 101 "la tua Fisica." The passages in the "Sacred Poem" are of course not only "quotations" like those in the *Convivio* and other prose works of Dante, but they show in a paradigmatic way and with deep poetical feeling how Aristotle and his doctrine are connected with Dante's ascent to heaven.

34. See Dante, *Divina Commedia*, Inferno, Canto XV, 85. Literally translated the line says: "You taught me how man makes himself eternal." The commentators of Dante, a great number of whom

I have looked up, take these words as meaning the attainment of literary fame or worldly fame in general. But the word *eterno* is always used by Dante in the most strict sense and not loosely as the traditional interpretation understands it here. That rule suffers no exception. *S'eternar* therefore must be referred to what Dante elsewhere calls *le cose eterne.*

35. See about Aristotle's *Nicomachean Ethics* as the source of Brunetto Latini's *Il Tesoro,* in the ethical part of the work, the book by Thor Sundby, the outstanding Danish authority on the complicated problem of Brunetto's literary sources, *Della vita e delle opere di Brunetto Latini* (translated into Italian by R. Renier, Florence 1884) p. 139 f. Brunetto even made a new translation of the *Nicomachean Ethics* from the Latin compendium, in which the work was mostly read by that time, into Italian. The editions of that translation to which Sundby refers on p. 139 and 140 of his book are not accessible to me in the Harvard College Library. Before Brunetto's translation the *Ethics,* or rather the above mentioned *Compendium Alexandrinorum,* had been rendered into Italian from the Latin translation of Hermann the German by the Florentine Hippocratist Maestro Taddeo. The Latin text of the *Compendium Alexandrinorum* which Hermann had translated from the Arabic is printed in Concetto Marchesi, *L'Etica Nicomachea nella tradizione latina Medievale* (Messina, 1904) pp. XLI-LXXXVI.

36. Aristotle, *Nicomachean Ethics,* X, 7, 1077 b 31: "*Man* must not, as the poets tell us, strive for *human things* nor, because he is *mortal,* attend only to *mortal things,* but he should make himself *divine* (ἀθανατίζειν, intransitive, i.e., to pursue a divine life) as far as possible. This is done according to Aristotle by the 'divine part of man,' the intellect. Dante could find this passage either in the Latin text of the *Compendium* of the *Ethics* or in Brunetto's translation of it. The Latin words are (Marchesi l.c. p. LXXXIII): "Non decet igitur ut sit desiderium *hominis* aut ipsius sollicitudo *humana* neque eius appetitus *mortalis* et si ipse mortalis appareat, immo *conetur ad immortalitatem* iuxta sue possibilitatem nature, et semper contendat ad vivendum vita nobiliore que est in ipso." Dante knew this famous passage of the *Ethics* and loved it as we can prove by his quotation of it in *Convivio* IV, XII, 8: "E però dice Aristotile nel decimo de l' Etica, contra Simonide poeta parlando, *che l'uomo si dee traere a le divine cose* quanto può." This can be attained only by the noblest part of man's nature according to Aristotle i.e. the intellect, as Dante quotes on one of the following pages. Being the actuality of man's intellectual abilities, the science of the eternal things brings human nature to its fulfilment. *S'eternar* therefore is the most fitting description of the supreme aim of human education. Dante's reference to the Greek poet Simonides proves that he took this passage of the *Ethics* from St. Thomas' Commentary; for Aristotle him-

self does not mention Simonides here, but St. Thomas does mention him in his explanation of the passage of the *Ethics* (p. 668, #2107, ed. Marietti). St. Thomas took the name of Simonides, as he says himself, from the *Metaphysics* of Aristotle (I, 2, 982 b 30). Dante quotes St. Thomas' Commentaries on Aristotle several times in his *Convivio,* including that on the *Ethics.* His words "*m'insegnavate come l'uom' s'eterna*" characterize Brunetto Latini as the master who has fulfilled his task in the true sense of Aristotle and St. Thomas. He has shown Dante in his youth the path which leads to the eternal things. The passage of the *Ethics* occurs also in Brunetto's *Tesoro,* Book VI, chapter 54. It thus appears that Dante's attention was directed to the passage first by Brunetto, either through his teaching or his work or both, and then he looked it up in St. Thomas' Commentary later.

37. The originator of this new "humanism" was F. C. S. Schiller in Oxford in his book *Humanism, Philosophical Essays* (2nd ed. London, 1912). Schiller referred to the pragmatism of William James as the immediate source of his thought, although in a certain sense his humanism claimed to go back to Immanuel Kant's *Critique of Practical Reason,* the book which in modern times established against the classical philosophical tradition of theoretical metaphysics the primacy of practical reason. William James, so far as I know, did not adopt the name humanism for his philosophy.

38. The comparison of the new philosophical "humanism" with the sophist Protagoras was made by its own author, see F. C. S. Schiller, *Humanism* p. XXI; see also the same author's *Studies in Humanism* (London 1907) Essays II, XIII-XIV and his pamphlet, *Plato or Protagoras?* (Oxford, 1908). One of the essays of his book *Humanism* is entitled: "From Plato to Protagoras."

39. See my book *Paideia,* vol. I, p. 298-299.

40. But see E. K. Rand, "The Humanism of Cicero" in *Proceedings of the American Philosophical Society,* vol. LXXI (1932) p. 207-216 (especially p. 213). Rand rightly points out that Cicero's humanism, in spite of his Academic restraint in matters of metaphysical knowledge, has a definite religious undertone.

41. This view about the origin of humanism is so widespread in philological literature that I need not refer to individual publications. See the first chapter on Isocrates in my *Paideia* Vol. III which is to appear soon, especially footnotes 2 and 5.

42. I must refer here to Louis J. A. Mercier's *The Challenge of Humanism* (New York, 1933) as another attempt at liberating humanism from the rule of naturalism and reasserting the position which was taken with so great success and promise by the late Irving Babbitt and his followers at Harvard University. See also William P. King, *Humanism* (Nashville, 1931) who surveys the

various forms of what is called humanism in American philosophy and their attitude towards the religious problem.

43. The *paideia* of Socrates and Plato is treated in the second volume of my work *Paideia* which will be published by the Oxford University Press in New York, 1943. See also the formulation of the problem in the chapter on the sophists in *Paideia* I p. 299.

44. About the following historical development see the extensive analysis in *Paideia* I, especially the chapters on the sophists, on Euripides, Aristophanes and Thucydides, and for the tragic poets the respective chapters.

45. The word *theology* occurs for the first time in Plato's *Republic* II 379a where Plato sets forth for his ideal state "outlines of theology" to be respected by poets and authors who in their works want to make statements about the gods and their nature. It is the task of this philosophical theology to determine the nature of God. From Plato's word *theologîa* Aristotle's term *theologikḗ* is derived. It is very likely, however, that this term was used frequently in the philosophical language of Plato's Academy, for the thing which is meant by the word was always in the center of discussion in that circle. We learn this from Plato's later works, and it is confirmed by what we hear from and about the other pupils of Plato.

46. Augustinus, *De civitate Dei,* VIII c. 4 f. Meister Eckhart (ed. F. Pfeiffer, Leipzig, 1857) p. 261, 21. I owe this reference to Ananda K. Coomaraswamy who also refers to Plato the words p. 130, 17, "Unser eltisten meister einen, der die wârheit ie vant lange unde lange vor gotes gebürte."

47. It is a wide-spread prejudice of the nineteenth century that theology was an oriental plant since the religion of the Greeks was "entirely undogmatic." The popular religion of the Greeks was undogmatic indeed, but the dogma and the doctrine, in short all rational theology, came nevertheless from the Greeks. It originated in Greek philosophy. It should not be overlooked that, historically speaking, Greek philosophy was the greatest creation of the Greek mind in the religious field. It has survived the popular religion of the Greeks for thousands of years and in this form the Greek genius will probably last as long as human culture.

48. Aristotle, *Metaphysics* VI, 1, 1026 a 19.

49. See the well known statement of Herodotus II, 53 that the old poets, Homer and Hesiod, gave the Greek nation its gods and were the authors of the prevailing views about their origin, names, honors, inventions and form. That is exactly what later Greek philosophers called mythical theology (*theologia fabulosa*).

50. Augustinus, *De civitate Dei,* VIII c. 2.

51. It is impossible to give here in detail my reasons for attributing to the pre-Socratic philosophers this important place in the development of the rational theology of the Greeks. I have dealt with this problem in a separate book on the *Theology of the Early Greek Philosophers* (The Gifford Lectures of 1936 at the University of St. Andrews, Scotland) which is not yet published.

52. For the interpretation of Socrates and Plato given in the text of this lecture see *Paideia,* vol. II.

53. Plato, *Republic,* VI, 511 b.

54. Plato, *Laws,* IV, 716 c.

55. Plato gives this metaphysical definition or redefinition of *paideia* (culture, education) in the famous image of the cave-dwellers at the beginning of book VII of his *Republic* (see particularly the introductory words of book VII about the philosophical aim of that comparison). "Conversion" (in Greek, *metastrophé* or *periagogé* i.e. turning one's head and facing in the opposite direction) is a philosophical term which Plato invented in order to describe the turning of the soul from the world of opinion and error to the principle of true being and the effect of this act on human life and personality. See *Paideia,* vol. II, p. 295 f. The term "conversion" which lent itself very naturally to the description of the religious experience of those who turned to the Christian faith was taken over from Plato by the Fathers of the Church.

56. Plato, *Theaetetus* 176 b. The definition occurs also in Plato's *Republic* X, 613 b.

57. Plato, *Laws* I, 645 a-c.

58. Plato, *Republic* IX, 592 b says that his ideal state exists only in heaven. His *paideia* is the "conversion" of the individual soul from the world of relativity to the absolute goal which is the center of that ideal state.

59. See *Paideia,* vol. III, the chapter on Plato's *Laws,* p. 242-261.

60. Aristotle, *Metaphysics* XII, c. 6-10 and VI, 1, 1026 a 19. See my *Aristotle* (Oxford, 1934) p. 131 f., 138 and 216 f.

61. Augustinus, *De civitate Dei* VIII c. 1.

62. See above p. 46 and Note 45.

63. Gregorii Nysseni Opera, vol. II, ed. W. Jaeger (Berlin, 1922) p. 271, 19, see also p. 270, 21-23.

64. In his lost dialogue *Hortensius* Cicero drew most of his philosophical arguments from Aristotle's exhortation to philosophy, the *Protrepticus;* see Jacob Bernays, *Die Dialoge des Aristoteles* (Berlin, 1863) p. 116 f. Concerning the *Hortensius* which made a profound impression on St. Augustine's mind and became a turning point in his religious development, see the famous words *Confessiones* III, 4, and the passage referring back to this event in his life VIII, 7.

65. C. N. Cochrane, in his stimulating book, *Christianity and Classical Culture* (Oxford, 1940) is not vitally concerned with philosophy as the greatest intellectual power which prepared the world for Christianity in the Roman empire. That this is also a gap in H. Lietzmann's *History of the Early Church* has been rightly observed by such an expert as was Eduard Schwartz in his review of the book.

66. *Acta Apost.* 17, 28. "For we are also His offspring" (i.e. God's offspring) is quoted from the Hellenistic poet Aratus (*Phaenomena* 5). The Stoic philosopher, Cleanthes, who was the source of Aratus for this line speaks of man as the offspring of Zeus in his celebrated hymn in honor of the highest god (v. 5). The author of *Acts* draws a parallel between St. Paul in Athens and Socrates in 17, 20. There the Athenian philosophers who come to listen to the apostle asked him to tell them of his new dectrine since they had heard that he wanted to introduce "some strange new ideas." This is an allusion to the accusation made against Socrates that he was introducing new deities or, in Plato's later terminology, a new theology. Plato, of course, agrees with this accusation and sees in it Socrates' historical greatness.

67. *Acta Philippi* c. 8 (3), *Acta Apostolorum Apocrypha* ed. Lipsius-Bonnet, vol. II, 2 (Leipzig, 1903) p. 5, 2.

68. Ps. Justin., *Or. ad gentiles* c. 5.

69. Ps. Justin., *De monarchia* c. 1. The author's aim in this book is to combine and reconcile what he calls the *humanistic* and the *religious* viewpoint in order to commend Christianity to the readers for whom he is writing. His words "philanthropos" and "philotheos" have clearly that meaning. As we have pointed out on p. 21, it is a common misunderstanding, even in modern times, to render *humanitas* (in the cultural sense) by "philanthropy." But the author shows how old this misunderstanding is. He says in c. 1 that his mind is religious (philotheos) but his form is humanistic (philanthropos). "Philanthropos" here apparently has the sense of formal culture. The author wants to give that humanistic form a new and better content with his religious idea.

70. Aristotle, *Metaphysics* I, 2, 982 b 28-983 a 11.

71. Aristotle, *Nic. Eth.*, X, 7, 1177 b 34, see above p. 35 and Note 36.